Penny Treasure

Complete Guide To Big $ Pennies Found In Change
By Sam Sommer

Copyright, Legal Notice and Disclaimer

This publication is protected under the US Copyright Act of 1976 and all other applicable international, federal, state and local laws, and all rights are reserved, including resale rights: you are not allowed to give or sell this Guide to anyone else.

Please note that much of this publication is based on personal experience and anecdotal evidence. Although the author and publisher have made every reasonable attempt to achieve complete accuracy of the content in this Guide, they assume no responsibility for errors or omissions. Also, you should use this information as you see fit, and at your own risk. Your particular situation may not be exactly suited to the examples illustrated here; in fact, it's likely that they won't be the same, and you should adjust your use of the information and recommendations accordingly.

Any trademarks, service marks, product names or named features are assumed to be the property of their respective owners, and are used only for reference. There is no implied endorsement if I use one of these terms. All images in this Guide are readily available in various places on the Internet and believed to be in public domain. Images used are believed to be used within the author's and publisher's rights according to the U.S. Copyright Fair Use Act (title 17, U.S. Code.)

Finally, use your head. Nothing in this Guide is intended to replace common sense, legal, medical or other professional advice, and is meant to inform and entertain the reader. So have fun and best of luck to you.

Copyright © 2017 Sam Sommer All rights reserved worldwide.

Contents

Copyright, Legal Notice and Disclaimer

Introduction: Did Michael Tremonti Get Lucky? An Ocean Full Of Pennies

Chapter One: The Lincoln Head Cent (1909-Present)

Chapter Two: The Lincoln Head Penny As A Collectible

Chapter Three: The Lincoln Head Penny Errors

Chapter Four: The Memorial Cents

Chapter Five: Where Do I Find Pennies?

Chapter Six: Getting Started

Chapter Seven: Review Of Terms and Errors

Chapter Eight: Finding A Good Coin

Chapter Nine: Children and Pennies

Appendix: Source Material - Error Chart

Did Michael Tremonti Get Lucky?

In 1969 the US Mint Made 261,311,510 pennies at its San Francisco plant. Michael Tremonti found one that had double features on the front. All the lettering and numbers looked like they were printed twice, slightly off center. His penny was one of only 25 like this ever found and because it was in uncirculated condition it sold for $ 126,500. But you have to ask yourself, how could only 25 double die coins been made? The answer is that there are lots more out there waiting to be found. Out of over 261 millions pennies made in 1969 there have to be more coins like this. The fact is that very few people look for them because they are not aware of what to look for and it gets even better than this. Just imagine how many error coins like this have been made for other penny years. The answer may surprise you!

Here's a close up look at the penny. Notice the doubling of the numbers, the S and the words "IN GOD WE TRUST". (The "S" Stands For San Francisco)

An Ocean Full Of Valuable Pennies

That's right. There are thousands, perhaps millions of error pennies that are worth hundreds and even thousands of dollars. Where then does one begin? What do you look for? Can you really be successful at this? The answer is a resounding "YES" to this question! Let's start at the beginning.

While there are many error coins out there for other denominations, the penny is a really good coin to start with. The reason is that there are so many error pennies that it is almost impossible to fail if you follow simple guide lines. The penny has been minted since 1793. While finding very old coins can be challenging, you may be surprised at the results you will experience once you get into this fun and profitable undertaking. It's not uncommon to find pennies over 100 years old in change. Also, people tend to ignore the lonely penny. After all, its only worth a "Penny"!

For practical purposes it is best to focus on Lincoln Head Pennies. Pennies earlier than this, such as Indian Head Pennies, very rarely turn up in change. Often referred to as small cents, because pennies minted before 1856 were quite large in size, the Indian Heads were minted from 1856 – 1908 and the Lincoln Heads from 1909 - today. Here are some examples:

Notice the three larger pennies on the left compared to the smaller pennies on the right: the Lincoln Head Penny and the Indian Head Penny.

The Lincoln Head Cent (1909-Present)

This penny type is one of the most sought after coins, yet very few look for error varieties. It's hard to give a good reason for this, especially when you consider that they are easy to find, and often worth much more than the non error pennies collectors seem interested in. In fact, the most valuable Lincoln Penny of the whole series, the 1909 S VDB (The VDB stands for Victor D. Brenner, the designer) is only worth several thousand dollars in uncirculated condition. When you consider that there are numerous error pennies worth tens and sometimes hundreds of thousands of dollars, the interest stays focused on the non error coins. And so the door opens for us, those looking for the error varieties.

When the Lincoln Penny was first minted in 1909 the designer's initials (VDB) could be found on the back of the coin at the bottom. Starting in 1910 these initials were taken off the coin. The back of the penny had a wheat design and is often referred to as wheat pennies. The Front Has The Bust Of Abraham Lincoln

Notice The Back Of The 1909 Lincoln Penny With The Initials "VDB" on it:

Starting in 1959 the back of the Lincoln Penny was changed from the wheat design pictured below to include a picture of the Lincoln Memorial.

In 2009 a special addition penny was minted to include four backs or reverses:

In 2010 the design was changed to its current reverse, the shield:

The Lincoln Penny has always had the same front and size, so it is easy to know what you are looking at – a Lincoln Penny. In addition to the design changes the metal used to mint the penny has changed over the years. This is important information and the reason will become clear later. In 1943, in order to save on copper for the war effort, the Treasury used zinc-coated steel to make cents. These coins are very attractive but have little value unless they are in very good condition.

Notice the gray color of the steel. High quality coins may fetch $20 or more.

In 1982 the Treasury decided to change the metal composition of the Lincoln Penny to a zinc alloy instead of 95% copper. It is made of 97.5 % zinc and coated with a thin copper layer. During this transitional year both zinc and copper pennies were made. A copper penny weighs 3.11 grams. A zinc penny weighs 2.5 grams. An inexpensive gram scale that detects to the hundred weight is a wise investment for detecting penny weights. For under $10, Amazon has this one: American Weigh AWS-100 Precision Pocket Scale 100 x 0.01g. Notice it weighs in 100th of a gram. When using it place a tissue on the scale before placing a coin on it so the surface of the scale does not scratch.

Please note that in 2009 when the Lincoln Cents were minted to celebrate the 100th anniversary of the penny some varieties were made of copper. These copper pennies were sold in sets to collectors. There is a drop test you can perform to determine if a penny is copper or zinc by listening to the sound it makes. Do not use this method. It is not reliable and some people have hearing that is defective and have trouble with tones.

The web site www.coinflation.com shows the daily value of coins with respect to their metal content. As of this writing, copper pennies are worth 2.3 cents each. It may not sound like a lot but when you consider that you can find several hundred copper pennies in a $25 box of rolled coins you are doubling your money. They are worth collecting and selling on eBay.

Here is a sample recent eBay auction: $100 Face Value 95% Copper Penny Bullion 68 LBS Sold for $ 174.52 # 370723890105 That's a profit of $74.52. Not bad for pennies that no one wants. This is a large amount of pennies. You can sell much smaller amounts and make a good profit. You might question how to ship 68 pounds of pennies. The USPS has flat rate boxes that can hold up to 70 lbs for one low price. These priority boxes get there in 2-3 days. So you can cover your shipping cost by charging a flat rate to all bidders, say $10. This auction was for 1500 copper pennies or $15 worth and it sold for: $24.50 – 1500 Pennies Pre 1982 Sold For $24.50

Please note: One pound of copper pennies contains 146 coins

The subject of copper pennies was worth mentioning. While it it time consuming, if you are already looking at pennies for their error value, why not set aside copper for sale on eBay for a nice profit. Or have your children save them for their future education. While copper is often referred to as "Poor Man's Gold", there is real gold to be found in these pennies.

Try this on for size: In 2010, a business executive paid $1.7 million for a 1943 penny made of copper rather than the zinc-coated steel used that year to conserve copper for World War II. Notice the copper rather than the gray steel color:

The Lincoln Head Penny As A Collectible

While the focus of this ebook is on Lincoln Penny errors it is important to take a brief look at the collectible value of the penny dating from 1909 – present. This is worth noting because while your are looking at pennies for their error value you might come across dated coins valued at several dollars or more that should be kept.

The value of any coin, whether it is an error or just an old coin, is directly related to the condition of the coin. Coins are graded by condition. The condition can make the coin go from just one penny to many thousands of dollars. So when you look at coins, those in good condition should be saved and evaluated. This link on grading coins can be helpful:

www.coins.about.com/od/coingrading/qt/coin_grading101.htm

For the coin collecting value of pennies refer to: The Official Red Book: A Guide Book of U.S. Coins 2014 [Spiral-bound]. Amazon sells it for around $10. The values in this book only serve as a guide. The coins can often fetch much more money at auction than the prices listed. This book is a valuable tool to have in your coin hunting arsenal. Don't leave home without it! You never know when you might come across some pennies and you have a chance to buy some. You can't pay for them unless you know what they are worth.

NOTE: Never buy a valuable coin unless it has been graded by a professional coin grading service that guarantees it is genuine and shows its grade.

There are thousands of fake coins out there and China is notorious for flooding the market with counterfeit coins, so be careful. Two headed coins are a good example of a fake magician trick type coin.

The Lincoln Head Penny Errors

There are literally thousands of Lincoln error coins out there. If you follow a simple step by step process, looking for them will be fun, exciting and rewarding. The types of errors you will encounter fall into two categories. The first type involves mechanical mishaps. An example would be when a coin is minted off center or the front of the coin is not in line with the back of the coin. Let's look at the most common ones so you know what to look for:

Off Center Strikes: Notice how the penny is off center.

Dies and Cuds: Notice the extra metal on the top of the coin

Rotated Reverse: The front of the coin is straight up and down but when you flip the coin over the back is angled to the side. The greater the angle the greater the value!

Clipped Planchets: A piece of the coin was cut off during the mint process.

Coin Blanks: One or both sides of the coin are blank

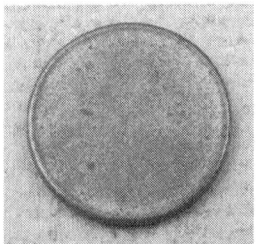

Lamination Errors: The top layer is peeling or was not stuck to the coin properly

Broadstrikes:

The coin is outside or not in the collar – similar to off center coins

When searching for penny errors you will encounter these mechanical errors. In order to determine their value please refer to this web site for great charts and values:

www.coinsite.com/html/userrorprices.asp

The value of your coin is relative to the degree of error and the condition of the coin. Coins with very noticeable errors have more value and coins that are in good condition have more value. These charts are only guides. You may get more than the chart value. In addition to these mechanical errors there are errors that are not so easy to spot but have tremendous value. They involve major mistakes that occur when the coin is minted and the numbers and letters are pressed on. Examples are double-dies also called double lettering and double numbers, wrong blanks used for the coin (penny printed on dime blank), and mules (right front wrong back).

The remainder of this ebook will focus on these error types and the reason for this is the belief that for the time you spend you will receive the greatest financial reward by focusing on these errors.
Remember: There are many fakes out there – so be wary of anyone selling a coin!
Let's look at some close up pictures of examples to get a feel for it:

Notice that in this 1955 double die the front of the coin has doubling on all the letters and numbers. Also shown is a closeup of the date. This coin in good condition is worth over $2000.

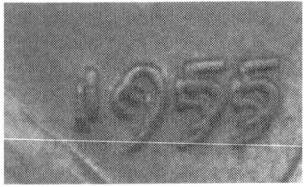

Here are pictures of a very rare mule – the front of the coin does not match the back. A penny front with a dime back: This coin is worth well over $100,000.

Getting Started

With millions of pennies in circulation it may seem daunting to figure out how to get started. Actually it is really quite easy and costs almost nothing. Before we cover the topic of how to get pennies let's take a close look at the most common errors that should be looked for. Please note that this ebook covers many of the errors but not all of them. Web sites listing others will be furnished later. The purpose here is to list coins that you have a good chance of finding. When a coin is listed we show an example of it when possible, but keep in mind that for any given error there may be variations. For example, in one error type the coin may have a doubling in the date and in another error type the same dated coin may have the word "Trust" doubled, so when we list these errors always look at the entire coin front and back, closely.

Coins the Treasury mint come from Denver, Philadelphia, San Francisco and West Point. Pennies with no letter under the date come from Philadelphia. Coins with a "D" under the date come from Denver. The "S" coins come from San Francisco. There are no West Point pennies. West Point usually mints gold coins. This picture above shows a D for Denver. Had it been blank it would be Philadelphia, an S means San Francisco:

One of the first Lincoln Head penny errors and one we will look at is the 1917 Double Die Obverse (front): Notice the doubling of the word "Trust".

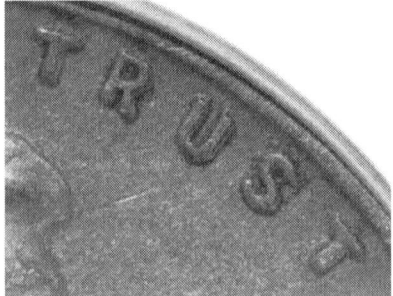

Worth anywhere from $200 on up, it is worth looking for when you search through boxes of pennies and old penny jars.

Another early coin that is of interest is the 1936 Double Die Obverse. It is worth from $25 to over $300: Notice the doubling on the date. There are several variations of doubling on the front, so look at the entire coin. The 1941 Double Die Penny: Notice doubling on the word "Trust"

Earlier it was mentioned that the 1943 copper penny was minted in steel because copper was needed for the war effort. A few coins however were made of copper and silver by mistake. Worth over $100,000 they should be looked for. They are easy to spot as copper looks very different than gray colored steel and it is magnetic. In 1944 the mint went back to copper, yet a few coins were accidentally made of steel. Again they are worth over $100,000.

In 1943 some steel pennies from the Denver mint had a doubled "D" for Denver and are worth from $25 to over $1000: Notice the extra D showing under the D. There is also a double die for the 1943 coin with no letter on it.

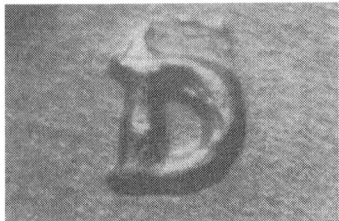

The 1944 D over S coin is worth from $125 to over $650: Notice the faint S under the D. The 1944S with S over D is another error you may come across and is worth from $35 to over $200. It is the only S over D in the entire penny set. The 1953 Double D Coin: Notice the D over the D

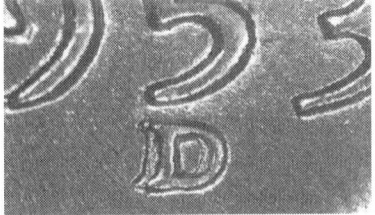

The S over D

The 1955 Double Die Obverse is a famous coin and has drawn lots of attention. Exactly how many were made is the subject of speculation. Some say that 24,000 were minted. It is quite valuable and is worth from $1500 to over $15,000 depending upon condition. In this coin there is doubling of the entire front. There are many fakes out there. Some coins have limited doubling, say part of the date. These have little value.

1955 DDO (Double Die Obverse)

The 1955 S over S Coin: Notice the two S's

In 1958 a few double die obverse coins were minted. Only three are known to exist but there are more out there. It is hard to put a price on it. Very rare.

In 1959 the Denver Mint made a mistake and issued a penny with a wheat reverse instead of the new memorial reverse. Only one has been found. Very valuable if found:

The Memorial Cents

In 1959 The US Mint changed the wheat penny reverse to the memorial reverse as stated earlier. Error coins mentioned so far were wheat back pennies that are older and harder to find but one never knows what you may come across so it is worth having this information.

In 1960 the Mint made a small date coin and a large dated coin. The Denver mint issued some "D" coins with an error. One D was put over another D making it worth from $50 – over $500. There are several variations of this error. There are also several types of double dated and doubled lettered coins for 1960.

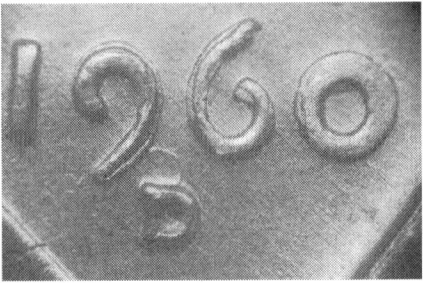

The 1960's saw other error coins made so keep an eye out for them:

1961 D with a second D under the top D $10 - $100 Value

1962 Double Die Obverse with doubling in the date and the lettering $10 - $30 Value

1963 D Double Die Obverse with traces of a second three in the date 1963 - $10 value

1964 Double Die Reverse with the "L" in the word Liberty doubled and some doubling in "In God We Trust". Value $5 - $15

1964 Double Die Obverse with doubling in "United States of America" From $20 - $90
Several types of 1964 DDO exist

1968 Double or repunched D $ 8 - $50

1969 D with a missing "FG" $2 - $10 See pictures: Notice the designer's initials on the top coin located at the right steps of the Lincoln Memorial. The bottom coin has no initials by the steps. Only coins with the initials completely missing have value.

The 1969 S Double Die Obverse. As mentioned earlier, this coin is worth many thousands of dollars. Here are some more pictures:

The 70's decade had its share of errors:

1970 D Double Die Obverse – doubling in the date $3 - $10

1970 S Doubled Mint Mark – The S is repunched $3 - $12

In 1970 the mint issued a large date and small date version. There are several good error coins associated with this date:

There is the 1970 D with a repunched D and a 1970 D double die obverse. The DDO shows doubling in the date. It is slight. The value for these coins is $3 - $12.

The 1970 S has a repunched S version and a double die obverse with slight date doubling. Again these are worth $3 - $12.

There is a 1970 S Large Date Double Die Obverse with strong letter doubling and doubling in the date, especially the "0" in 1970. This coin is very valuable and can easily bring in as much as $25,000! Notice the strong doubling in the phrase "In God We Trust".

Another version is the 1970 S small date DDO. It is worth less and has some doubling in the "TY" of Liberty and the 7 in 1970. Value is $15 - $50. The small date 1970 S can be distinguished from the large date by looking at the 1970.

In the small date version the 1970 is lined up on top, while the large date version has a 7 that is lower than the rest of the numbers. In general, 1970 S small date coins have value and should be saved.

In 1971 two double die obverse coins were minted. One is much more valuable and it has strong doubling on the phrase "In God We Trust". The other has much weaker doubling. The valuable one is worth $ 70 - $2000. The less valuable one is worth $30 - $70.

The 1972 coin has over 15 different types of double die obverses. Some have minor doubling, so you must inspect every 1972 penny very carefully. They are worth from $5 – over $10,000!
Here are two of the more valuable ones: The coin pictured below can fetch $10,000. It is referred to as variety # 4. Notice the doubling of the G and O.

This version called variety # 1 has very strong doubling but is worth less: $80 - $500.

A 1972 S coin has a DDO (Double Die Obverse) version and is worth $35 - $150. Strong doubling on "In God We Trust".

A 1980 DDO coin is worth $60 - $400. The date has doubling – weak so look carefully.

In 1982 a large date and small date coin was minted. A large date version has some doubling on the word "God" and "We". Worth about $30.

In 1983 coins had several double die versions. Version # 1 has very noticeable doubling and is shown below, while version # 2 is less obvious. Both however are worth as much as $350.

Another 1983 coin with value has very noticeable errors and is easy to spot. It can bring in as much as $750. Notice the big piece of metal on the reverse side.

In 1984 an interesting error occurred. It seems that the US Mint decided to give Lincoln an extra ear. There are several types, some with a big extra ear and some with smaller ear parts. It can sell for as much as $250. This picture is showing the big extra ear. Notice the secondary ear below the main ear:

Another 1984 coin has doubling on the date and lettering and is worth $25 - $70.

Please Note: Coins minted from 1983 to 1989 had some major errors with respect to the "D" mint mark. It seems that many of them were repunched or printed twice. They have some value $7 - $25. Look closely at the D.

In 1988 the designer initials "FG" located at the bottom right to the Lincoln Memorial steps on the back of the coin were minted in extra heavy or thick style. The letter "G" in particular is very bold. Value of $45 - $180. Also happened with the 1988 D coin.

FG vs **FG**

In 1989 some coins had a doubling next to the columns of the Lincoln Memorial. It appears as extra metal running vertically next to some or one of the columns. This also occurred in 1991, 1994 and with the 1995 D coins. Notice the extra metal next to the last column on the right. This extra metal can appear in any column and can be strong or weak in appearance. Value varies from $10 to over $250.

A 1995 coin had strong doubling of the lettering on the front of the coin and is worth $12 - $75. This also occurred with the 1995 D coin but the D version is worth much more, from $ 125 - $500.

A 1996 Double Die Obverse has some doubling on the date and the letters "RU" and "ST". Look closely because it is subtle. A value of $125 - $675 makes it worth looking for.

In 1997 another "Double Ear" coin appears and is worth from $45 - $ 150.

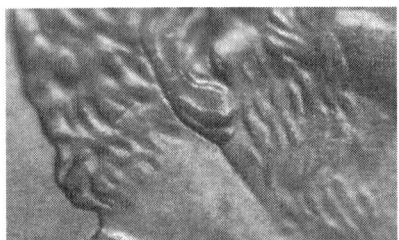

In 1992 a major error occurred and it repeated itself in more years. The first type appears in 1992 and is called the closed "AM" The letters in America, particularly the "A" and the "M" are so close together they are almost touching each other. This happened for the 1992 D coin as well. Worth many thousands of dollars and worth looking for.

In 1998 another error like this made the letters "AM" too wide from each other, the opposite of the 1992. Much less valuable $ 1.5 - $50. In 1999 another wide variety was made and is worth more $150 - $1000. Also in 2000 a wide variety was minted, valued from $ 1 - $45.

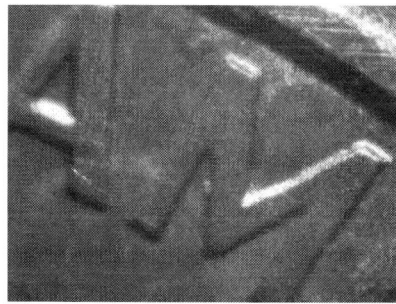

In the 2000 decade several errors occurred.
A 2001 Double Die Obverse with extra thick letters – the "RTY" of LIBERTY.
Valued at $50 on up to $300.

In 2003 slight notching of the same letters "RTY" brings a value of $15 - $100.

The 2004 coin had a double die front and back with the letters on the LIBERTY showing slight notching and thick lettering on "UNITED STATES OF AMERICA". This coin is worth $50 - $300.

Also in 2004 some coins had doubling on the reverse side, the "E PLURIBUS UNUM" is extra thick on one type and the other has doubling of the letters "E PLUIBUS UNUM". Worth from $10 - $100.

In 2004 and 2006 remnants of a second ear appear below the primary ear. The 2004 coin is valued at $10 - $75 and the 2006 coin is worth as much as $150.

A 2006 double die obverse has nice doubling on the word "LIBERTY" and is worth up to $350.

For many 2009 coins an extra finger and thumb show up making these coins worth up to $50. Notice the second thumb showing up. Also look for extra fingers.

In 1983 an unusual error occurred. This was the first year that the copper penny was no longer made of copper. It was made of zinc with a very thin copper layer on top as we mentioned earlier. That did not stop the US Mint from making some copper versions by mistake and if you find one it can be worth $15,000 or more. So you can weigh all the 1983 pennies you find. If it weighs 3.11 grams instead of 2.5 you're in luck.

Where Do I Find Pennies?

Pennies are everywhere. They come from old penny jars, piggy banks, loose change, coin holders (collections) and from banks in loose form or rolled form. It does not hurt to ask around for old pennies from friends, country stores, flee markets, yard sales, etc…It is important to mention that the majority of the population has a big misconception regarding older pennies. For some reason they think that because they are old they have great value. This is not true. The age has little to do with it. What is important is the condition of the coin and the rarity of the coin. This is important information so you do not pay too much if you come across an old penny jar and your friend wants $20 for $10 worth of pennies, claiming that they are old. Do not pay it unless when you look it over you see some really old coins, say more than 100 years old.

If you notice that the coins are very shinny, in good condition, this could make them more valuable. For practical purposes it is best to order a box of pennies from your bank. Make sure they do not charge you for this. Most banks will provide the $25 box containing 10,000 pennies for $25. Some banks try to charge a fee for this service. If your bank does, have a little talk with them. If they do not want to work with you find another bank. Ask the new bank what they charge for rolled coins and tell them you want to open a savings account and if you do will they get you rolled coins without a fee.

A $25 box of pennies has 50 rolls and weighs about 14 pounds. It takes the bank several days to get the box in. You can also buy loose pennies the bank may have. People turn in penny rolls all the time looking for cash instead of holding onto pennies.

There are two tools you will need when looking through your pennies. One is a box of nitrile gloves. These are non latex and non powdered gloves that you must use because coins are very dirty. Amazon has boxes of 100 gloves for under $10. The other important tool you will use is a 20X or 30X magnifying loupe. This one found on Amazon is under $5: SE Illuminated Loupe with LED Light – 20X from Hobbytoolsupply. Make sure you get one that is illuminated. Buy two of them. They contain a small battery.

You cannot search for coin errors without a magnifier. When you receive your penny box of 50 rolls start with one roll. Use a small screw driver to pry it open or hit it on the edge of your table to break it open. Do not re roll coins. Banks have heavy duty plastic coin deposit bags they supply for free. They cost the bank about 75 cents. If they want to charge you, they can be found on line for as little as 60 cents each. As you go through your coins keep track of how many you set aside so when you get ready to bring the bag back to your bank for deposit you will know how many pennies it has. Make sure you write your name and account number on the bag.

Getting Started

Rather than feel over whelmed by so much information, let's review and create a step by step approach to this. When you look at pennies the first thing you want to check is their mechanical condition. Does the front and back line up vertically? Is the coin off center? Does the coin look different? Is the lamination peeling? Is there extra metal or is a piece of the coin missing? Anything unusual should cause you to set the coin aside for further evaluation.

Next you will check the condition of each coin. Newly minted coins will be very shinny but when you find older coins that are shinny you should set them aside. Coins with old dates, say over 50 years old should be set aside. You will find foreign coins and sometimes dimes. If the dime is old, set it aside. Foreign coins have no value.

What about error coins? Since this is the primary reason for your searching you must have a list of error coins so you can easily spot dates of interest. So whenever you come across a 1983 penny, for example, you should weigh it to see if it is made of copper. If you spot a 2009 penny, for example, with the reverse of Lincoln reading a book, you should look for extra fingers.

Review of Terms and Errors:

A coin with just a date and no "D" or "S" under the date is a coin that was minted in Philadelphia. A coin that has a "D" under the date was minted in Denver. An "S" means San Francisco. The term DDO or Double Die Obverse means that somewhere on the **front** of the coin numbers or letters or words have some form of doubling, they were hit twice. The doubling can be very noticeable or very faint. You must look closely at the whole coin. When we say a coin is D over D or S over S we mean that the mint mark shows up twice, similar to a repunched mint mark. In some years pennies were made of the wrong material and these are worth a small fortune. You have to weigh some coins to find this out. Some dates are called small dates and some coins for the same year had bigger dates. The date is small on some coins and bigger on others. Some coin error years had many variations of the same error. So on one coin the word "Trust" may be doubled and on another coin the date may be doubled, for example. In other words look over the whole coin. Some coins had missing designer initials – the "FG" is missing. On some coins the "FG" is too faint and on others it is too bold. On some coins there are extra fingers, extra columns, extra ears. Some coins have the "AM" of AMERICA too close and some have it too far apart.

Finding A Good Coin

No doubt you will come across some valuable coins. If you suspect the coin is worth $100 or more it is advisable to have it professionally graded so you know for sure what it is and what it is worth. There are many good companies that perform this service and their fees are minimal. Call them first before sending in a coin. Here are some examples. Compare price and service:

- ANACS

- Collector's Universe

- Independent Coin Graders

- NGC

These companies certify that your coin is the real deal and then grade the coin so you know what condition it is in. This service helps you sell your coin. No one will buy a valuable coin unless they are certain it is what you say it is. It's like an art dealer looking at your painting and telling you it is real and what it is worth.

If you decide to sell your coins, eBay is a good platform for this. If you are not familiar with how it works we have developed a step by step system to assist you. Please refer to our book: Silver Coins: How To Find Silver In Pocket Change (Secrets Revealed). It has an incredible eBay course in it and other info that will help you make extra money. The small investment will pay off in a big way! Thank you and best of luck in your treasure search. You never know what story can be found concerning that lonely penny you come across.

Children And Pennies

The best way to get children involved in coin searching is to buy them a box of pennies when you get your pennies. They'll feel important having their own coins to work with as you work with yours. Most children love the excitement of searching for a penny worth as much as a car!

> **WARNING: Coins--especially pennies--are a major choking hazard for children under the age of four. When handling coins, children should be supervised and wearing latex gloves at all times.**

As your children collect pennies and find copper, talk with them about counting, using, and saving money. Make their coin searching into a fun educational experience. Older children can practice their math skills by calculating and writing down the age of the oldest penny in each box. Or they can calculate the age difference between two pennies. Younger children can use pennies to practice counting or perform simple arithmetic. There are many other kids games with coins that are suitable for children of all ages.

Children can use pennies to learn how to weigh objects. As mentioned, pennies have different weights depending on whether they were minted of zinc or copper. Have them weigh each penny and separate them by metal and mint date.

> **If you have a child ages 5 to 10, The Financial Fairy Tales Treasure Box is an inspirational series of fun books written to help kids learn the value of money and create successful lives.**

For only $4.99, Amazon.com has a great Whitman coin folder called Lincoln Cents for Kids: 1979-2012 Collector's Lincoln Cent Folder [Hardcover]. It holds pennies from 1979 to 2012 and includes lots of interesting educational facts about our nation, its land, and its people. Amazon.com also sells coin folders for pre-1979 pennies.

Source Material

The internet has good source material for Lincoln errors: www.lincolncentresource.com and http://www.coppercoins.com/advsearch.php are of particular interest. Many good books are also available. Ken Potter's book: "Strike It Reach With Pocket Change", is highly recommended. Amazon has it for around $10 in used format or Kindle format. A new 4th edition is out now. Remember that many, but not all, error coins for Lincoln Head Pennies are listed in this ebook "Penny Treasure". The major ones have been listed and described.

Other books of interest:

"A Detailed Analysis of Lincoln Cent Varieties" By Billy Crawford
"The Complete Guide to Lincoln Cents" By David Lange
"The Authoritative Reference on Lincoln Cents" By John Wexler and Kevin Flynn

Use This Chart When Looking For Errors

Having this quick reference list will help   * - Very Valuable

1. 1917 DDO (Double Die Obverse)
2. 1936 DDO
3. 1941 DDO
4. 1943 D over D
5. 1943 Copper Penny *
6. 1944 Steel Penny *
7. 1944 D over S
8. 1953 Double D
9. 1955 DDO *
10. 1955 S over S
11. 1958 DDO *
12. 1959 Wheat Back *
13. 1960 Double D
14. 1960 DDO
15. 1962 DDO
16. 1963 DDO
17. 1964 DDR (Reverse)
18. 1968 Double D
19. 1969 D Missing "FG"
20. 1969 S DDO *
21. 1970 DDO
22. 1970 D – DDO
23. 1970 S DDO
24. 1970 D over D
25. 1970 S over S
26. 1970 S Large Date DDO
27. 1970 S Small Date DDO
28. 1971 DDO
29. 1972 DDO (15 Types)
30. 1972 S DDO
31. 1980 DDO
32. 1982 DDO Large Date
33. 1983 DDO
34. 1983 Copper *
35. 1984 Double Ear
36. 1983 D – 1989 D Double "D"
37. 1988 Thick "FG"
38. 1989, 91, 94, 95D Extra Columns
39. 1995 DDO
40. 1995 D DDO
41. 1996 DDO
42. 1997 Double Ear
43. 1992 Closed "AM" *
44. 1992 D Closed "AM" *
45. 1998, 1999, 2000 Open "AM"
46. 2001 DDO
47. 2003 DDO
48. 2004 DD Front/Back
49. 2004, 2006 Second Ear
50. 2006 DDO
51. 2009 Extra Fingers

Made in the USA
Las Vegas, NV
09 November 2022